FRUITLANDS

Thank you to the editors of the following publications, in which some of these poems first appeared: *Bay Poetics*, *Bird Dog*, *Commonweal*, *Five Fingers Review*, *Mirage #4*, *Shampoo*, *The MAG* and *Xantippe*. Thank you also to Ugly Duckling Presse and A Rest Press for supporting this work.

Many thanks to the valuable readers of these poems in earlier stages, to my family for their support, to Todd for his ear, and most of all to Rusty — for all that and everything else.

ISBN: 0-9723331-9-3

Typesetting & book design: E. Tracy Grinnell
Cover photo: Orchard House c.1865. Courtesy of the Louisa May Alcott Memorial Association.

Litmus Press is funded by Ether Sea Projects, Inc., a 501(c)(3) non-profit organization. Contributions are greatly appreciated and tax-deductible to the extent allowed by law.

Litmus Press
P.O. Box 25526
Brooklyn, New York 11202-5526

Distributed by Small Press Distribution
1341 Seventh Street
Berkeley, CA 94710
www.spdbooks.org

KATE COLBY

FRUITLANDS

LITMUS PRESS
BROOKLYN • 2006

CONTENTS

for Ruth Taft Hamilton

A BODY DRAWN BY ITS OWN MEMORY

1

Certain labels are impervious
to solvents, impermeable
as drawn bridges.

Adherents are bound
to bridge and tunnel
around
                    columns

                    of figures
                    playbills
                    newsprint
                    and smoke
                    dispelled
                    by the wind

                    in Stovepipe Town.

2

Tall buildings tip on casters
or are counter-
weighted
(also by the lurid light of subways).
Dust gathers on the wainscoting.

She runs a hand around a column
marbled
with the spectral pain
of amputees

Containing decomposure
in dividing cells, abiding
effacement
the door plaques and pediments
engraved with dispelled words.

Concentric desire outspreads
her strained connectives;

she's diaphanous,
dazed and diffused,
flecked like fake marble.

      3

There's a devotion called unflagging
to seeing oneself in surfaces—
in a window, a shadow, a standard,
or the immediate space around another body.
She rubs against the space between them,
like that of repellant magnets.

And he does his part in words
with the sound of empty
soda bottles.

4

As a child on the stoop,
she traced her tarsals,
sucked the bend of her elbow.
Some parts of herself she's forgotten,
though others who've loved her
know them better.

This case-based knowledge replaced
by a longing spiral on a spinning disk

pushing outward from an empty center.

5

a mackerel sky   descending

PANGAEA REDIVIVUS / RE[AS]SEMBLING ANASTASIA

It is later labeled drift, but we feel the centrifugal force of it. A tectonic wish fulfillment, maybe; the fissures contain the satisfaction of throwing a puzzle at the wall. Oceans creep in.

What lies between: a monogram, an instep, a dirty stocking in Berlin? Puzzling equations. For example, you were learning French, while I was busy trying to forget it. We study the shifty blue hearts of flames, the shifting blue borders of our allegiances. You in Prussia, mapping your *terra incognita* with a hoe and compass, planting posts, plotting coordinates of discontinuity.

Charting courses, dodging icebergs, or we are taking in and passing water like an aquifer. Let's become amphibious, I say. You say: this language will get us nowhere.

She walks the perimeter with a dousing rod and compass, detecting instabilities, possibilities, predicts a sinkhole behind the house.

In a three-wheeled cart she slakes desire, cartographically; consumes an atlas, maps boundaries between which the earth's foundries are sealing cracks. Assembling forgeries.

The earth cracks with lack of rain. She peers inside at blue flames, but will not be swallowed today.

What lies between: a Prussian beet farm and itself? They call it steppe, or a topography of no relief.

A drought. Throughout Bororwihlas the peasants are on their rooftops, tearing off thatch to feed to the livestock. They'll replace it with something less permeable.

Still: she is made of drifting plates. She is no longer allowed to wash the dishes because she tends to let every third fall and break. She pieces them back together into relief maps. Patterns interrupted, she can finally read them.

She has thrown away her needles and the mice are making progress, busily gnawing through her threads. They are gnawing through the third leg of her three-legged stool. She is beginning to list, to drift into uncharted waters; Pangaea *redivivus*, she redistributes the weight of a globe.

The glue only holds so long; the plate maps crumble over time, fall into pieces, archipelagos.

Where is the rent? demands Doris Wingender. Doris is a seamstress.

Stockings steam before the fire, shed skins, perforated, her skin is full of rents and holes that grow by the day. Sometimes her foot rips straight through and leaves the torn skins flapping at her ankles.

She staggers through the streets like Charlie Chaplin, flayed bits of her waving like adjectives and misplaced punctuation.

Doris is glowering from the top of the stairs. The fire's glow casts shadows on her face, but this, too, is just a trick of flames. Doris casts no shadows; she inhabits herself like a point.

Here, the blue hearts of flames like blowtorches or the entropic potential of a munitions factory. She holds a grenade in her hand, like Atlas, a globe.

She is holding up the assembly line, but through the smoke and sparks the other workers can't see what she's revealing.

She is Pangaea; she'll smash this globe like a plate against the wall.

Here, at the center of the earth, the heat and magma make her giddy. *Magna est veritas*. She tips her hand, the globe falls and her neighbor explodes in protest. He drips from the ceiling, bits of flesh cling to her face.

She's also taught herself a bit of Latin.

Where is my sister? Felix wants to know, and heads off with a stringy, starving dog. He finds Franziska, ear to the ground. This piece of earth will heave and wind up elsewhere; she's never felt more at home than at the center of this subduction zone.

Of this purgatory: she's been consuming an atlas, whose definitions she can't digest. She eats dirt by the handful, chokes down soil, rubies, tropical meridians and boardwalks of Yalta. She once savored them like glue.

And she is digging, digging mines at their feet. This is shaky ground. Felix returns to tilling beets and leaves his sister to her undoing. To her purgation—or a pyroclastic wish fulfillment. She vomits earth, parallels, cheap paper borders and expectations steeped in beet juice like blood.

The stringy dog lies down to die beside her and their skin and hair become caked with dust. They cover their heads and wait to be swallowed.

We are moving forward in metes and bounds. In cadastral surveys of consciousness, we read our beginnings and endings, but plumb what lies between.

She lies in bed reading maps. Shaky fingers tracing borders, plotting coordinates of neither nor or boundaries between: Poland, Russia, Germany, a farm, a factory, a western front of uniforms and empires like aquifers, in pigeon holes or dialects of accretion and self-ablation. Bloodlines, *belles lettres*. An impossible dialectic. They used to say she put on airs, but she longed for layers, like petticoats of what else.

She inhabits her bed like a black hole, performing her last right, lengthening ceiling shadows in blue flames. Her last intention. She stays in bed withholding intention and omissions that collapse as holes in sand. The earthquakes contain themselves in points; there will be no reverberations like onetime waves of lovers. She once used them for glue.

She once imagined bridges and last-chance migrations, revisions. But she's thrown away her flimsy needles; Pangaea is coming apart at the seams. Oceans creep in.

A foggy night of Berlin. Franziska walks the outskirts with a dousing rod and compass, burning bridges, her bootlaces flapping like lips of hooked flounder. On a bridge over the canal she stops to pull her shawl over her head and in the lamplight the water below ripples like blue hearts of flames.

Crouching on the wall, the equator, and below, the flames between desire and what was never meant. She releases the dousing rod, watches as it's swallowed by the canal. Her element, her solution.

And leaning forward, she's now taking in and passing water like an aquifer. Her last rite or wish fulfillment.

She'll be an anemone, inhabit undercurrents. Her eyes are opaque blue marbles.

GEMINATION

It often starts with a white night. A cartoon biology of cells peels away from the checkered linoleum—you coming with? Girls in white nighties fly upstairs and leap into bed and the positions arrange themselves before us into rule tables of computational complexity. Let's assume that the squares have smoothed their lines and angles into blobs. This way, we can understand emergence as a function of gentle amoebas rather than conspiratorial boxes. But the amoebas are still black and white; about this I can do nothing.

We begin to lose distinction between the hardware and the process and the amoebas are clearly acting according to Class Four rules. The girls pull the covers over their heads and we squint our eyes, looking for the parameter, the critical value that will determine the system's behavior and the likelihood of extended transients. The parameter is always derived from the rule itself.

□

A blue cafeteria with tables that fold down from the wall. Assemblies are also held here and the principal claps his hands for attention. Flat backdrop of a fifth grade play.

Friday is taco day with a stale shell and shreds of pallid lettuce. Ice cream sandwiches.

SLIDE

You and I inhabit thresholds, clinging to neither here nor there, and to
and: this is a threshold of no relief, of interrogative light and obviated
shadows, of questions flattened between clapboard slides,
in laboratories of hanging frames — in a potential frame,
the next moment slumps beneath the shadow of the overhang.

They call it earthquake weather, a day like this, of reflected light
and leveling heat of no relief, of corners around which
and angles of incidence jellied in consommé,
molded in amber lunches of tea and
impossibles: no incidents or tension, no reflection.

No striations; rather, a bangle, a broken shoelace
and what are we going to do about that hair?

We were in a boat. You were navigating and I was tending
the lines, which flew from my hands, flapping like live wires
on the wind. You watched the shadow of our sail on the water
through the light reflected in your face, conducted a depth sounding:

You went under, but not overboard, swam away to plot reliefs
of ocean floors. It is far too shallow here to die.

for Chip Madden

FRUIT OF THE SEASON'S SLUSH FUND

Being that
she's always to be found
in space made by concertina wire
a drab and tattering habit fashioned
by many charming seasons

> (the gray sound of spokes
> yelled *deuce* behind the baseline—
> courted trapping in a tennis skirt)

For what it's worth, preferring
a third, green rail, fifth wheel,
wrenched at the rhumb line, scabs
pushing barbs, ragged paths by what passes
for a pick-up in the night.

Picked up and driven home:
the Post Road pitted with sown salt, hitching
posts adrift in dirty snow
and stonewalling
in the rearview mirror, a semblance
of permafrost
making all shoes insensible.

Let down, rather
than recoiled
from time
in time for the local pandemic

of porchlight, inoculating
a revival of whist
under the weather.

What's more:
her paper fan-shaped frock
unfolding
into little dead places.

AFTER DINNER DIASPORA

With a sticky wicket
forfended in departure
her flight pattern forecast
on the steamy lawn.

      blinking
      planes and shuttle-cocks
      rise above the privet

It was the sideboard dispenser
and the weather-fretted shed,
the chromatic stacks and fricatives;
a half-hexagonal window bay.

The Prince of Wales was married
the year
the days were stacked
in icebox cake,
the candle wax at the wayside,
in tonal colonial
blue.

It was the guttering stubs and stopgaps
in a bucket by the door.
It was the sound of covered bridges.

Breaking form
and falling
out of line as into
another empty cup of tea
posed her question on the table—
you   are   excused.

                                    After all
                          the second guesses,
              echoes cracked her *contrapposto*;
        he played slap string with his back
                          turned and bent
    like the arch under which they were married.

DISTRUST IN RETROSPECTION, OR
THERE'S SOMETHING IN THE SENTRY BOX

In a damp and enchanting
crescent
I practiced seeing the desert.
But sand took the form of
stone and soon
everything there was becoming
in a round-about way

    being taken by the following:

        a busker peddling
        with sticky fingers and a habit
        of elaboration,
        a credible period ruffle.

It was evensong on the cattle road
and halfway round there's a war on
            or more likely just a rustle
            a rooking in the thicket.

Launching missives at the Old Mitre:

      Now we're in the thick of it   *and*   *that doggerel,*
          I can't get the lines
              out of my head

        The dairymaid
        The alderney

The gray light through the clerestory;
fragments were falling, all of a piece,
recorded and spiral-
bound to backpedal
at breakfast induced by news

The marmalade
The certainly
The taking of
The liberty

Changing guard at Whitehall,
traded desert for shoring and gained
a tea gown
for slapdash deposition staked
on other hallowed ground.
The pomp and currency were layered
in half-completed
coffee rings.

(defrocked
in a punt up the river:
a drive of digging
your stick in the
mud.)

FALSE SPRING

1

OVER THE TRANSOM

(Definition)
>   a rich yellow ochre
>   on a dark red ground

Apportioned by theories of relativity
spattering grapeshot indicia
of the *parvenu manqué*

>   a banana republic
>   conceived in dictation

>   the output a measure
>   of the rage
>   addled imagery of put-upon
>   and singular influence
>   of single most importance

It took him twenty years.

2

HIS FAVORITE FATA MORGANA

She practiced a form and later adopted.
Put out.
He worked.
She remained at heart.

3

UNDER THE RADAR

Beneath the range as cost
of her deliverance

      a clear red fading
      into another ground

If there is only one claim
in a company town,
one is this, else
sharecropped,
cut to another's sizing.

She delivers in impressions

      turning into
      something else.

4

THE WILL-O'-THE-WISP

From all the crevices in the floor,
from all the moldings, from every recess
there grew slim shoots filling the gray air
with a filigree of leaves: a hot-house jungle,
full of whispers and flicking lights.

THE FOLD

Barring self-reference
       "the ultimate violation"
in soft assemblies of fine lines
netted, having half a mind
to reduce to semi-
second paper *demimonde*
of dripping,
blood-letted light let to seep
till the parallel takes
shot at the bloody whites of their eyes
                          nodding

to break at will.

Being of two minds

She cared for vegetation only when it grew
here and there among ruins.

Along high tension lines
between figure and ground,
the alternation, generation
buzz of a bellwether
heat is straining utilities

breakers tripped
by taxation,
representation,
double negative
of politicos engaged
in clean-up

Counter to curvature,
it's an awkward pose,
but the camera always adds weight.

a unit of housing conceals
remnants of a parapet
in the dooryard
a rake

a lamppost's worth   rusty staples   radiate & amass   a discomfiting heap
under the bed   of events distended   and conforming discomfort.

Meter readers collect on hand
washing, sidewalk hours
of glassy reflection and admiration
of *millefeuille* and trumpet flowers.

There's a hyperbaric forecast
        (someone's left the faucet on
                        to
                a *well-turned phrase*
hotwire takes, turns over,
resumes the rolling blackouts.

A platform is isomorphic, flanking
tracks, injection-molded boxcars
cast a constant
racked and hacking death-rattle

hackneyed industrial   watermark
at tide line of uniform notation

a rutted, muddy road   is trees   tapped   is sap   indistinguishable
from water   boiled down to   form, fuse   & break   a real, old-timey
sugar bucket   rafter accent   six cords burning   (wampum)   questions
marks   what to stick in your yard

They would use their tomahawks to make incisions in the trees,
then insert reeds and run the sap into birch bark buckets.

hair is shingled for summer
the iron retired till fall
when curls come round again

Having no remedy
for paradox
of private information, fiber-
optic imprimatur is worn and strung
with ribbon for the latest constellation—

Bang and capitulate.

Autology leads to
recapped circulation
tapped and sclerotic,
what's wrong with this
sentence: self-reference
of a black hole.

UNTITLED TRIPTYCH

Weaving spiders come not here.

□

There were three discrete spaces of habitation there. Some might have called this superimposition, such terms of subsequence making common epithets. But the edges were there, if only in effigy. And the rules were simple, being simply of relativity, of time passing more slowly in a moving frame than in one that was stationary. In homage and deference to this rule, a flat frame of Ionic columns had been laid over the landscape. The frame extended infinitely, laterally, in either direction. It was shifted by one square, three times daily.

In deference to other rules they had not yet written, the members typically gathered on the lower edge of the frame. The frame had a semblance of steps, despite its want of a third dimension. And there they lingered, enjoying their thusly-extended pastimes, their thermidor and their revisionist musical reviews.

Accordingly, we were all equally squared away, the rule also being that things that are equal to the same are equal.

□

In deference to the content, the entire setup had a sepia cast. And yes, I intend to include the actors, both we and those gamboling on the superstructure. The monochrome trees and clouds had been smeared in such a way as to indicate intactness from without, though the dissimulation was apparent to all those of us contained therewith. The trees and clouds in truth secreted only absences behind the columns, the roughly sawed-off portions serving as reminders to us of the necessity of the arrangements made. For those recently arrived, these jagged edges suggested a promise. But, once shown the ropes, one saw how formations were so often finished, denatured. We took to dissolution, making moonshine in the blank spaces, huddled and marveling at the health of the two-dimensional.

□

Still, the green, green grass, even with the cast, was enchanting. And even more so, the wondering of what was on the other side, was it even greener: were we in or out?

The landscape was concave; this was apparent. Upon arrival, one's inclination was to leave the scene entirely by gaining Square Four, but such was an impossible geometry. New subjects would spend the first days clinging to the marginal squares, but would relent in due course and roll back to Square One. Square Four afforded a position of privilege only in its diagnosis of the sidelines.

This is what gets you: Square Four is made of smooth, white plastic. .

Proving that derivation is a cousin of the proof.

A LOOMING DEPENDENCE ON WEATHER

Provability is a weaker notion than truth.
—DOUGLAS HOFSTADTER

1

One knows of
stockpiled liver spots,
catalogs and creeper
practically
wrapped around the newel post

        the stand of ash
        in the wind
        the floor is
        green and flickering

An early gray gathers as it goes,
means the body that made the work,
later turns to gold,
things filtered by leaves:
air, light, chewed pen cap
through the bitten window
new mown hay is growing.

2

Scene from a Yard of Toile

A gold ground with a red impression:

the woman tends   to washing linens   brook-   side   roughly
pounds them against a board   not stirring up   silt   against another
reflex   deadened by disuse   mobcap cladding   to be slapped
clean on the morrow   clotheslined   on the rickety   paling

A boy sows seeds.
A second leans
against a leafy tree
bent
to the sound   of his music
                              straining
and so forth.

3

Lady Lovelace is at the harmonium
weaving leitmotifs
of colored leaves
that fall and amass
in a masterpiece of counterpoint.

But precipitates fall and take form
as haystacks
of fretted gold thread unbinding the code

      there's a hole
      where
      she doesn't know

                a lashing   picture window
                     gathers
             shadow on the wickerwork

Untoward sharps and flats
settle in the spaces of her staving.

At the same time she is wresting.

The rests denote a floating.

                A gathering
                dusk
                dust falls
                phragmites in the corner.

MERIDIAN

Turning to
weightless
implements
of gear-click
hedging in

      instamatic

      blue, our ticking
      gaze
      in light
      like waves,
      overturning

A lifeline,
a forerunning wake of life
rafts and instruments,
liminal seconds
in cesium
skimmed threshold
or eleventh hour

      draped
      across
      the doorjamb.

We lack fear of flatness
or our impalement
on axes, blinking
a reticle of stasis;
turn it over and begin
again, this dripping
like TV test patterns.

Let's stay, I say,
and buoy ourselves
in river locks
intercalated
in channels
or our fender-bent
synapses, recycling

this floating.

Never believing in water torture or autisms as misfortune,
we were counting gold in a pointillistic landscape of radiating
boulevards. In Budapest, a necropolis of shifting foci grid-dots,
Soviet heroes, missing limbs.

The thought does not sadden us,
but the calculation
of sundials;
whether flat or equatorial

they always deliver

this sublimating ice

(we are tapping on the ceiling)

FOUR REFLECTIONS

1

Claptrap reflections,
or nothing lies
the first time around.

In binocular trafficking
of pools
in badlands shadow
and pinhole flats,
a lightning field
of poles.

2

Rosetta stone of desert floors
draws vapor clouds and mesas,
cataracts of exile,
where firmament meets figuration,
a tablature of erasure.

The golden calf melts into its reflection—

Coming down from the mount,
Moses cups water in his hands.
He sees the people in it.

3

Reflection as aphasia
where distortion parts seas.

A hothouse of cell walls distended
with chlorophyll, unconsummated,
these dead-ended intentions.

And this light like fireflies
battering cupped hands.
Pinholes of tiny eclipses.

4

Your letters read like crop circles
in a boundless field of green.

Or, on a glassy sea a ship runs into a rock.
The sky a boundless blue screen, flickering,
the intonations of immortality.
And our skin crawls
with mites,
which we brush off in favor of;

   such that, peering over the edge,
   the mirroring sea becomes us.

GRAFT

a gathering of tables
a round which

   (leap seconds
   jam between   leaves
        un-
           fitting

four days short of
sidereal crumbs in
saucers as wide eyes
trace dust motes
of a solar day, now
eleven short of loony.

We lay linoleum over the floorboards,
in counters of ingraining. And preferring
equinoctial lines on plastic, we always
get to *The Times* a day late.

Our eternal hoarding;
        in a box under the stairs,
          "Pieces of String too Small to be Useful."

On a wall of morning glories
espaliered
we'd read them splayed
and stripped in the evening.

Grafting in moonlight:
the triteness befits
a tuning of fork
to impossible plane.

       Scions in juice
       jars force
       roots on the windowsill.

A SORT OF ZERO DEGREE HAIRCUT

*If you really wished to go unnoticed, you would be back where
you started.*

—ROLAND BARTHES

Supposing the letter
and fascinated
with charity

        spoon-fed singularity
        defines the point
        of no derivative
        for any given function.

Flights are taken
two at a time

        Oo the banisters,
        a beautiful Victorian
tenement   scrolled in dirty greens and blues

        why
        Paris in the pictures! pegged
        a brown silk cloche and another
lapidary trail   left by a finger in the dust.

                     □

Fixed on the way
the mouths move at museum cafés
one bellies up and leans there   all night long.

□

Are you all over
the perennial revival? said
while lifting the prestige
of the first French sailors.

You were wearing stripes for the sake of it,
as morphology and vocation
contained between the lines

neutrality as the sign of neutrality

      that, and the postcards
      of famous paintings.

THE COLLAPSIBLE TELESCOPE

Start wide, expand further, and never look back.
— ARNOLD SCHWARZENEGGER

1

A leading man learns the trade:
craft of watertight vessels, make-
shifting deadened weight and measures move
from hold to gunnel and back again

    Heels, ballasted with hollow plastic
    unseenly swinging from the rail
    no resistance, context, this jury-
    rigged
    to sway

with canonical modulation
and classic smokescreen heroes.

All rules waived   not rocking the boat

No object, distance,
need for a sextant,
the stars contracting
in epoch period pieces
authenticated
with frigate or diadem

found in sets of hammered tin
and walls with seams of safety glass.

2

(At the edge of a lake so deep
and still we called it Rorschach)

Playing the prefect,
hero in a greatcoat,
dusky bracken, full moon,
a piebald pointer chases its tail.

(Self-swallowing reflection behind the credits—)

      In favor of the figurative,
      but consumed by patchwork,
      the farceur flutters paper chains.

      (Scene One) a crystal ball
      reveals only its own interior
      of transubstantiated sand,
      leaded, dead and circuitous

      hocus corpus: here is my body

(Flash forward to final take of bullet casings on the beach)

3

Found recording on a wax cylinder:
He touched my breast (later modernly
denoted by a semi-circle)
in tracked feedback circuits of input.
Add spin for soothsaid comeuppance
in endless loops of stickball,
local, self-perpetuated and unslowing.

Gently lift the needle and add it to the stack
of dusty records gathering
on the attractive sectional furniture.

4

Runner-up for his favorite role,
but not to be outdone
by other pretenders
to figureheads and frigid wives.

The captain's raft
sucked into an eddy,
with rope and piton
wicked away
above the tide line
by forces gathered
and contracted
to lead him back
to Altaforte.

                    The peg-legged
                    lead the pegged
                    by the hand
                    and everyone
                    staggers in circles.

In the final scene,
noisily eats a piece of meat,
pounds his fists on the trestle —

He is in your corner.

LIPONYM

They were busily painting them red.

They felt the thorns of it and her in their sides recalling the crown
of and its disembodied purposes bleeding like hearts in the dust,
while he again, not the queen, though she always did prefer to hide
in rubies; has no use for fickle diamonds.

They wondered if he asked if they were red or white.

Was it the long stems, her cheeks, the wine, the slow dancing
and she wears colored glasses? The shade of itself is neither
here nor there and have you ever really seen one that color,
anyway, but no one's dared to say

the
same and
same and
similarly different referent
is a (is a) same
by any other name.

She's out for blood. Seeing red. They'll keep quiet and their heads.

TOWARD FRUITLANDS

There is alpine and alpine, either having
what to do with embroidery and knots,

steep roofs pitched against thin twigs
and radiant children singing the descant

in an opposing manner of clear, northern
light, streaming the forest green with needles.

Tinsel-headed Santa Lucia, stranded,
a crown wreathed with a crown of candles,

a white girl in a book on a white page, turned
a thin foil wrapper—of an Easter chocolate—

into a tiny aluminum dress, resembling
over a hundred others in a shoe box, turning

to a glowing paper chamber, if only not
the paper taking miasmic form of light,

discorporate form of a rice-paper lantern,
traversed and neither contained nor filled.

Following the ticker tape; it was New
Year's Day on Fifth Avenue of feeling

small, a small and snowy-looking German woman
stepped out of the crowd to tell me she loved

my hat (the wooly white one with the flower
that R gave me; wondering for the last two

weeks if it made me charming or ridiculous)
and I was charming and wore it well,

having the double edge of both embodying
and discorporating, neither of which is

disappointed on Fifth Avenue, where the plate
glass is already absorbing and opposing one

to one of many other unnecessary objects
of reflection, a paper flight toward Fruitlands is

already here. The original subjective correlative
in spades and bare hands. Could end

up here, having "Transcendental Wild Oats"
relate the first journey, wherein—this time—

the mother struggles with a mirror she's brought
to hang in the new house, and her husband

seizes it and smashes it against a fence, because
"there are to be no false reflections here." How

if the story has it that he has grown
an unsightly and iconographic beard,

which was not fashionable at the time and he
went to prison for defending it. The beard

is in line with the charming hat and the mirroring
plate glass and this needling problem, lately arranged

in mathematical terms of ratios or a simple state
of one-to-one. It is now several years after I first

attempted to figure the problem (not figure
out), which became necessary because I was
getting older and bleeding.

First Analogy

STEREO : MUSIC : : PROJECTOR :

Circuitry to sound of notation, an affection gathers more than one,
meaning from the note. Form is relation, ranging from complete identity
to mere thematic allusion. On the other hand. A marching band employs
methods of conveyance. The last three seats play Floyd, by which a stereo
has green vinyl and a girl denoting Kelly in an alpaca sweater. One-to-one.
The intercession of a soundboard is dividing, *La Vie en Rose* from a plate
of white asparagus. The smell of traffic. A quiet pew. His hands man the
stops, his feet, the bellows, and I was taking notes on the order of service,
e.g., "Sonya=God=*illumination!*" The black and white feeling of Franz and
passport stamps, as is the sound of "sortie" as isomorphic as is to broken
film, broken, even, flapping.

Answer: HER FLOOR HAD A FINER POLISH THAN ANY IN PARIS

The first figuration of the apparent perceptual disaster
was A—and continues to be so, if I'm going

to be honest—and a story I wrote about
visiting Uxmal and how the restoration

made the site less authentic—he, always looking
for absolute correlation, even at the risk of a

pickpocketing, which never happened, or not
then, but which seemed an apt example of what

A would risk in his search for ability to lie flat
against a fact and conform to it (the foil

on an Easter chocolate). Later, he was mugged at
gunpoint in Cambridge, beaten up in New Orleans,

suffered Post-Traumatic Stress. I was never at
Uxmal with A; I was with R, who doesn't go in

for armchair correlation, making him
more suited to pyramids than many others.

All he wanted was a questionable translation
of the petroglyphs, so that we could identify

the question. R's only overt role in the story
is the tweedy professor getting

high at the planetarium and wildly spinning
the stars around, which had something to do

with time and maybe relative degrees of civilization
as relative, but I might be revisioning why from

this other vantage point. The real reason was
that the A character wore a carefully worn leather

jacket and drove a carefully preserved orange Honda
motorcycle, which still signifies this hang-up on the

one-to-one. That we have. We three. And others,
who are mostly men, I venture. The reason

for Fruitlands, which really hooked me, *I trow*,
with Bronson Alcott disallowing the cankerworms

to be disrupted, and thus only allowing the inmates
to plant the sort of vegetables whose roots grew into

the air, which is—what—tubers? Wrong. Outmates.
To be so extreme is a privilege I hope never to enjoy;

somebody is missing. Upset. (Revised.) Let
down. Possibly this has happened: I spent

days in A's would-be *pied-à-terre* in Saint Germain,
drinking wine in the propped window and listening

to him diddle gravely on the guitar, after which
we'd go to bed, to a club, practice listening

to mid-'90s jazz. Another charming appropriation
had us seeing the Beastie Boys in the outskirts.

The crowd booed the opening band,
which made the Beastie Boys mad

and us disdainful, affording a beautiful one-to-one,
zero degree of separation from the Beastie Boys,

which might have gotten us backstage if we'd wanted
to play the national card. ("A finer polish

than any other in Paris.") To live off the land is still
to live off and to till to till, so this ontological Eldorado

of living with one's roots in the air, of those air plants
or performing inversions and staying there. Now,

Pangloss (everything?); a skipping syllogism
of optimism, perfection caused exchange of cause

and effect, e.g., the pants therefore the legs, making
it thoroughly sensible to sit on a pile of gold, rather

than weed the garden or tossing it out of car
windows or whatnot. You can have your tubers,

but can you eat them? There was another fellow
at Fruitlands who wanted to be rid of the digestive

tract all together (and a variety of blind
consumer whom A referred to as "food eaters,"

most often when he was high and engaged in same)
which is the turn in the story,

where one understands that the goal is simply
to fade away, not put down, wear unsullied

white while sweating —

Second Analogy

FORK : UTENSIL : : DOVE :

One-to-one-to-one or two-to-one as one of. A recursive method has much
to recommend it, though another might go with this and this and this
for snow. Return. What by way of tines, four-to-one, a fork has a utility to
the power of ten with a whole set and a horde of hungry Rationalists. But
here we have just one and a ration and a degree of removal from a dove.
While making sandwiches, why not cantilever a fork to a bird, which is the
wanted answer, I imagine, so bring it back to a dove. And forth to have a
road diverge and encounter a peacock. No, turkey.

Answer: FORK : BIRD

Return with a yellow vellum overlay of expensive
night out and an expensive notion of there having

been no way out, that this is what it means to be
"a friend," an eye for an eye rather than to

an eye together striking an impeccable wall
of cardboard bricks, made to look like bricks

—a recent memory I can apply to
the superfluity of intestines when one

refuses to digest and there's no one interested in
what you're regurgitating, i.e., "No one wants to hear /

what you dreamt about / unless you dreamt about /
them," which is a thing I've considered pointing out

to T, who's always recounting his dreams (and the
one about me had something to do with the two of us

driving into a brick wall!), but I don't because I always
want others' dreams to be just as interesting

as my own, to the extent that all minds turn
to slurry when there's want of attention; maybe

I should pay more attention to the suspended state I
take when T is relating dreams, but the problem is

the attention. It's attention affording discretion.
In the other room R is typing and through

the propped window there's a ladder and a rosebush
and a fence and I'm letting it slur so that they're

holding hands and dancing in a circle around me,
but I am the one ringing. In counterpoint. A *contre-*

temps performed *en pointe*, it was only after
many years of ballet classes that the terms began

fading through in English. I'd think, *"pas de chat"*
and suddenly see that I was able to execute

the movement because the words weren't referring
to anything other than the trajectories and speed of

my feet. Knowing French, I must have sub-willfully
held translation at arm's length in the interest

of creating a solely muscular—and variable—referent;
invoking a cat, I might not have heard the music,

or else have identified it as *mazourka* or *adagio*, thus
impeding the movement (I identify them as lines,

and now they are not coming very quickly at all). Here is
the equation I've made: starvation = dream life = dance,

or, reading the negative space: language = language
—we've all been there—

but to whack a new route up a different face is
a project, at least. How will I get there another day.

To get there again and again is all, refrain
(from making easy comparisons to Greek mythology,

cute terms you'd be wont to create, such as
"lexical crampons" or "perceptual piton" or other

journalistic reductions).

Third Analogy

RESTAURANT : FOOD : : POWER PLANT :

The product consuming the patron is made of metastasizing in an agent.
To make it fifty-fifty, when there are battlements of razor-sharp cliffs and
each is on the other side. To confer advantage would be far from me, to
one-to-one. There is earth and earth and a fork is neither a dove nor a
restaurant, but might have more to do with a plant. There is no fork, unless
the restaurant and a question of the figure and the ground; who's got the
information and where, which requires more equipment? A power plant
supplies beach pails by the bucket.

Answer: THE SET OF ALL SETS THAT IS A MEMBER OF ITSELF

Having only the necessity of turning
an impression into a renaissance fair, a woman

wore braids and purple velvet, the difference between
"harridan" and "termagant" is receding and has

everything to do with a dumb injunction against
the owner of a Boston bookstore, which I had no

right, according to my own code, to even read, but
to never cease to be amazed by violations of self-

description is not a poor place to be (another path
found—or taken). It was autumn and the leaves

swirled like a pot of liquid gold; dark fell early.
They ate beans from tin plates before the large,

stone fireplace, sat on logs. Rested their cold feet
against the andirons. At this time the discussion

turned to God and education. They rested their
cold feet against the andirons. Things began to

steam, then dissipate. My in-laws are Hare Krishnas.
They make soap and shun onions and teach Waldorf.

For awhile they lived outside Belfast, in a town
of mostly militant Protestants, except for

the militant Catholics and everyone claimed
his every curb, signpost and phone pole with

his colors of allegiance, allowing one to know
where everyone lived, because the neighborhoods

were painted either green, white and orange or blue,
white and red. Everyone knew who the Krishnas

were and were only vaguely interested in this
difference among them. Other than an incident

with a squirt gun, they were left alone. In [London]
Derry everyone picked fights with—they all looked

the same, thinking, it must be hard to know where
to lay the wire and train the telescopes. Carry the

tabernacle. Wailing wall. Learning the word
"anachronism" from "The Trojan Women,"

where in one scene an airplane flies overhead
and you can see the shadow on the ground, behind

Helen wringing her hands or washing her feet.
Iphigenia was led up to a very high altar to a

good deal of wailing below. Quasimodo sat in
a belfy, howled and swayed. All of this when I

was seventeen, a member of Students United
for Racial Equality, which deductively led all

of the girls to wear skimpy clothes to school one
day in protest of the verdict of a trial involving

a woman who'd "asked for it," and several
years before that, one of the more popular

Halloween costumes was "prostitute," which
gave other girls license to wear torn fishnets

and dark lipstick, requiring them to sneak out
and dress at another, more permissive parent's

house, one who didn't have to be told she was
going as a vagabond again. There's something

in this, too, of wanting to align oneself rather
than inhabit, which is why it was a great relief

to get to college and be Lana Turner simply
because one happened to have a gold lamé dress.

Rather than align, to have learned to inhabit,
in theory, by superimposition, is the best

way I've found to keep a mind out of / out of
the gutter. Emerson said, "They look well in

July. We shall see them in December." To grow
thin, hipbones merge with counterpane,

connectives melt and render one.
In December they will have learned about

the requirements for efficient production,
will have to either agree to the cattle and/or

the cattle being a book contest or exquisite
vase, hand-blown in Vermont and sold

on Newbury Street. Wearing DEET. Deferring
jury duty. He smacked his girlfriend on a

street corner, but was drunk and seems like
a nice guy. To let / let off requires some steam

NOTES

Page 12: Anna Anderson, *née* Franziska Schanzkowska, was the most famous pretender to the identity of Anastasia Romanov, the youngest daughter of the last Russian tsar. She was raised on a Prussian beet farm and briefly worked in a German munitions factory.

Page 21: Written after *Georgia Engelhard* by Alfred Stieglitz.

Page 26-27: Italicized lines beginning with "The dairymaid" are from "The King's Breakfast" by A.A. Milne.

Page 30: The text in part 4 was adapted from a passage in Bruno Schulz's short story, "The Tailors' Dummies."

Page 32: Italicized lines are from *Madame Bovary* by Gustav Flaubert.

Page 38: Written after *Untitled Triptych* by Gottardo Piazzoni. "Weaving spiders come not here" is the motto of The Bohemian Club—"the greatest men's party on earth," according to Herbert Hoover.

Page 43: Lady Ada Lovelace is credited by many with conceiving the first computer program, for Charles Babbage's Analytical Engine in 1843. She was also the daughter of Lord Byron.

Pages 58-71: Fruitlands was a Transcendentalist utopian community co-founded by Bronson Alcott in 1843 in Harvard, Massachusetts. The experiment failed after 7 months. Alcott's daughter, Louisa May Alcott, recounted the experience in a short story entitled "Transcendental Wild Oats," published in 1873.

Page 65: Quoted lines beginning "No one wants to hear..." from Built to Spill's "Made-Up Dreams," *Perfect from Now On*, 1997.

also by LITMUS PRESS

Danielle Collobert: Notebooks 1956-1978 (trans. Norma Cole)
Inner China, Eva Sjödin (trans. Jennifer Hayashida)
The Mudra, by Kerri Sonnenberg
Emptied of All Ships, by Stacy Szymaszek
Euclid Shudders, by Mark Tardi
The House Seen from Nowhere, by Keith Waldrop
Another Kind of Tenderness, by Xue Di (trans. Keith Waldrop, Forrest Gander, Sue Ellen Thompson, Theodore Deppe, Stephen Thomas & others)

Aufgabe, an annual journal of new American poetry and poetry in translation:
#1, eds. E. Tracy Grinnell & Peter Neufeld with guest editors Norma Cole and
    Leslie Scalapino
#2, ed. E. Tracy Grinnell with guest editor Rosmarie Waldrop
#3, ed. E. Tracy Grinnell with guest editor Jen Hofer
#4, ed. E. Tracy Grinnell with guest editor Sawako Nakayasu
#5, ed. E. Tracy Grinnell with guest editors Guy Bennett & Jalal El Hakmaoui

FOR MORE INFORMATION OR TO ORDER GO TO WWW.LITMUSPRESS.ORG

green press
INITIATIVE

Litmus Press is committed to preserving ancient forests and natural resources. We elected to print *Fruitlands* on 50% post consumer recycled paper, processed chlorine free. As a result, for this printing, we have saved:

2 trees (40' tall and 6-8" diameter)
785 gallons of water
316 kilowatt hours of electricity
87 pounds of solid waste
170 pounds of greenhouse gases

Litmus Press made this paper choice because our printer, Thomson-Shore, Inc., is a member of Green Press Initiative, a nonprofit program dedicated to supporting authors, publishers, and suppliers in their efforts to reduce their use of fiber obtained from endangered forests.

For more information, visit www.greenpressinitiative.org